NOW THAT'S BIG

GOLDEN GA

Published by Creative Education
P.O. Box 227, Mankato, Minnesota 56002
Creative Education is an imprint of The Creative Company
www.thecreativecompany.us

Design and Production by The Design Lab
Printed by Corporate Graphics in the United States of America

Photographs by Alamy (david sanger photography, Art Kowalsky, Ron
Niebrugge, Robert Harding Picture Library Ltd., Galen Rowell/Mountain
Light, Chris Sutton, Tom Tracy Photography, Underwood Archives),
Corbis (Bettmann), Getty Images (John Lamb), iStockphoto (Frank Van
Den Bergh)

Library of Congress Cataloging-in-Publication Data
Riggs, Kate.
Golden Gate Bridge / by Kate Riggs.
p. cm. — (Now that's big!)
Includes index.
ISBN 978-1-58341-704-1
1. Golden Gate Bridge (San Francisco, Calif.)—Juvenile literature. I. Title.
TG25.S225R54 2008   624.2'30979461—dc22   2007052340

CPSIA: 051910 PO1278

9 8 7 6 5 4 3 2

CREATIVE EDUCATION

TE BRIDGE

BY KATE RIGGS

Pacific

Ocean

San
Pablo
Bay

Golden Gate Strait →

San Francisco ●

● Oakland

San
Francisco
Bay

● San Jose

The Golden Gate Bridge is a long bridge. It is in San Francisco, California. The bridge goes across a strait called the Golden Gate.

The bridge had to be built one section at a time

6

In the 1920s, many people wanted to live in San Francisco. But it was too crowded in the city. People had to move to towns across the strait. Then they traveled on boats called ferries to get to San Francisco. An engineer named Joseph Strauss wanted to make traveling easier. He started building the Golden Gate Bridge in 1933.

The orange towers look like ladders reaching into the sky

8

Another man named Irving Morrow helped design the Golden Gate Bridge. He wanted to make the towers that held up the bridge look like steps on a ladder. People liked his ideas.

The Golden Gate links the ocean to San Francisco Bay

10

The Golden Gate is underneath the Golden Gate Bridge. Its water is 400 feet (122 m) deep.

Workers had to blast through rock to make room for the bridge. They had to swim deep under the water to plant the pillars in the ground. Then they had to build the roadway.

For 20 years, the Golden Gate Bridge was the largest suspension bridge in the world.

The Golden Gate Bridge was finished by May 27, 1937. About 200,000 people came to walk across it. It was 4,200 feet (1,280 m) long. Some people ate picnic lunches and danced on the bridge! People in San Francisco were proud of their bridge.

Most boats can go under the bridge's 220-foot-high (67 m) span

14

The Golden Gate Bridge is a bright orange color. Ships can see it from far away.

Fourteen years after the Golden Gate Bridge was built, a bad storm hurt the road. It was not safe for people to use. Workers had to make the bridge stronger.

More than 100,000 cars drive across the Golden Gate Bridge every day.

16

More than nine million people visit the Golden Gate Bridge every year. They can drive, bike, or walk across it. Sometimes there are lots of cars on the bridge. This slows people down.

Heavy fog is common in San Francisco, especially in summer

People can visit the bridge any time of the year. Winters in San Francisco are not too cold. And summers are not too hot. But strong winds, fog, and rain can happen at any time.

Keeping the bridge in good shape is a full-time job for about 55 painters and workers.

People who work on the bridge have to be very careful

The Golden Gate Bridge welcomes everyone to San Francisco. The big, orange bridge is a one-of-a-kind wonder!

In 1994, the Golden Gate Bridge was named one of the Seven Wonders of the United States.

22

GLOSSARY

design—*draw up plans for*

engineer—*someone who plans how things like bridges will be built*

pillars—*tall structures that help hold things up in the air*

strait—*a body of water that connects two larger bodies of water*

suspension—*when something is held in the air instead of being flat on the ground*

READ MORE ABOUT IT

Bunting, Eve. *Pop's Bridge*. New York: Harcourt Children's Books, 2006.

Murray, Julie. *Golden Gate Bridge*. Edina, Minn.: Abdo Publishing, 2002.

INDEX